CULT
PSYCHOLOGY

CONNOR WHITELEY

DEDICATION
Thank you to all my readers without I couldn't do what I love.

INTRODUCTION

I absolutely love cults.

Not only do cults provide the media, fiction writers, the news and lots of other forms of entertainment with an endless source of inspiration. But cults are extremely interesting to psychologists.

Because cults are very strange in terms of psychology. They make a person suppress their identity as the cult provides them with a new one. Cultists give up their autonomy and lots of other interesting findings have come around by investigating cults.

But not only will this book investigate cults and cult behaviour through social, cognitive and clinical psychology viewpoints. We'll also look at what a cult actually is (because let's face it entertainment can get this wrong) and we'll look at how you help people trapped in cults.

Of course, nothing in this book is any sort of professional advice but it's great to look at.

This book will be great!

Who Is This Book For?

Mainly aimed at university psychology students and psychology professionals, this book will give you a great in-depth overview of cult psychology as well as cult behaviour. So we can all begin to understand why and how cults work.

All explained in a great, engaging, easy to understand way.

You won't want to miss this book!

Who Am I?

I always like to know who's writing the nonfiction book I'm reading so I know the book is full of reliable information.

In case you're like me, I'm Connor Whiteley an author of over 40 books and 20 of these are psychology books. Including my best selling Forensic Psychology books.

Also, I'm a psychology student studying at the University of Kent, England.

Finally, I'm the host of the weekly The

Psychology World Podcast available on all major podcast apps and YouTube. Telling people about great psychology topics and psychology news.

Now we know what the book is about, let's dive into the great topic of cult psychology.

This is going to be fun!

PART ONE: THE BASICS OF CULT PSYCHOLOGY AND CULT LEADERS

BASICS OF CULT PSYCHOLOGY

As much as we all want to dive into 'proper' cult psychology, we really need to learn the basics first. And unlike a lot of psychology basics, the basics of cult psychology are very fun and worth a read.

But first, why is it important to learn about cult psychology?

Personally, I would love everyone to learn about cult psychology because by learning about cults, how they work and how to defend ourselves. This can help us keep ourselves, friends and family safe from cultic influence.

Vulnerability and Recruitment:

When it comes to cults, there is a very sad truth. No one joins a cult willingly. No one willingly chooses to give up their freedom and replace their lives with a superior leader that controls them.

Instead people are recruited into cults.

Now I understand if you're a bit confused by the distinction (I know I was at first). But the difference between willingly joining and being recruited by a cult is there's a lack of informed consent.

Another way to illustrate my point would be to imagine yourself wanting to join a cooking club. You love cooking, you love making friends and this cooking club doesn't try to influence you or control you. Then it's likely you'll willingly want to join it.

However, if this cooking club tries to influence you, use manipulation tactics and start brainwashing you. Then you aren't going to willingly join that. Instead you're been manipulated and recruited to join the cooking club.

As the treasurer for my university's baking society in 2020/21 that was a very scary idea.

So, how are people recruited by cults?

It mainly comes down to vulnerabilities due to a cult can easily learn someone's vulnerabilities and use them against them. As well as sadly everyone has different individual vulnerabilities. No one is perfect and this brings me back to the important point about learning cult psychology and tactics. Therefore, in case anyone tries to use these tactics and vulnerabilities against us. We can hopefully recognise and deal with the situation.

Some of these vulnerabilities are situational and others are internal. For example, the death of a loved one, moving to a new country, area or city, being on the Autism Spectrum, high hypnotisability and having strong active imagination are all vulnerabilities.

Interestingly, if a person makes excessive use of hypnosis, medication, drugs and other activities. Then this can actually induce an altered state of consciousness.

Overall, all these vulnerabilities increase a person's susceptibility to being recruited into a cult. And sadly chances are if someone does have a lot of these vulnerabilities then it is rather likely they will be recruited into a cult given the chance.

Unless the person has strong critical thinking, media literacy and a good supportive social network around them to keep them grounded.

In addition, what media literacy means is a person's ability to critically analyse, thinking and evaluate the source of the information.

Example of Media Literacy

Personally, I'm not afraid of making myself sound like a snob (I'm a very normal person in real life) but this is why I only read and trust two or three media outlets in the UK. As well as I don't read tabloids and they're very manipulative and I don't trust their reports.

Mainly because there was one article in a British Tabloid in 2021 trying to get people shocked and horrified that a woman spent £6,000 a month on living bills. At first, I agree that seems a lot and no one should spend that much money, surely?

Then I evaluated what the tabloid was saying and it mentioned the woman paid so much a month for a professional subscription. Just like psychologists, doctors and lawyers have to.

Overall, my point is this tabloid wanted to make people annoyed and shocked for no reason. Because this woman was almost certainly a high flying professional on at least £50,000 a month so to her and her partner £6,000 is probably not a lot.

Other Risks:

In addition, to the risks above, there are a number of risks that can increase a person's vulnerability to recruitment by a cult. For instance:

- Trauma
- Phobias
- Alcohol or drug problems
- Learning or communication disorders
- Unresolved sexual issues

A quick note on these other risk factors is trauma, learning or communication disorders and unresolved sexual issues can possibly all relate to a person's want for support and community. As well as sadly if a person is isolated and doesn't have a good social support network then a cult with all those members can seem rather tempting.

Furthermore, in more recent years, there has been new risk factors that we'll look in various ways later in the book. Thus, some 21st century risk factors are:

- Internet addiction
- Lack of touch, social distancing and isolation
- COVID-19 pandemic
- Severe economic disruption
- Increased time online

Overall, if a person is in a vulnerable state then they can fall for one of these many techniques and be recruited into a cult.

What Is a Cult?

After talking about the various vulnerabilities people have and how cults recruit people into their ranks. We need to define what is a cult?

I want to say up front that the word cult shouldn't be used lightly because as we'll see in a moment cults can have horrific consequences to the members. As well as a group shouldn't be called a cult because of its unorthodox beliefs.

For example, a new branch of a religion that believes in a more liberal approach to the religious teachings isn't necessarily a cult. Simply because of its unorthodox beliefs.

What a cult is, is it's usually authoritarian in nature and it's led by a person who has complete or almost complete control over its followers. And this all comes down to influence.

Cult Influence and Control

To be able to control a person, a cult must influence them and recruit them into the group. With the aim being the cult influence is designed to replace a person's identity with a new one.

Now, this is done in a lot of different ways and some of these tactics we will look at in the book.

However, each type of cult has different ways of acting and conducting themselves. Some types of cults are:

- Political
- Religious
- Large group awareness training
- Self-help
- Multilevel marketing

- Commercial
- Conspiracy theory
- Labour/ sex trafficking
- Mini-cult (family/ one-on-one)

Building upon this, different cults do things differently. For example a political cult focuses on influencing people through political means and drawing on their political beliefs. Whereas a self-help cult would draw on a person's desires for self-improvement and to better themselves.

Moreover, one of the biggest problems with trying to recognise influence is we're being influenced every single day and we're use to it. I talk more about persuasion and social influence in my Social Psychology book. But we're constantly being exposed to influence, and this can make it difficult to detect.

Here's some examples of sources of influences in everyday life:

- Business
- Psychotherapy
- Politics
- Religion
- Educating
- Media
- Relationship
- Parenting

Nonetheless, I do need to say influence can be positive and helpful. As seen in psychotherapy, educating and parenting. But influence can be detrimental too. For instance in some parenting, relationships and religion.

Undue and Due Influence

As I mentioned in the last section, some influence is good and other types are bad. Therefore, it's important to understand the difference and what's makes influence good or bad.

Which is where due (positive) and undue (negative) influences come in.

As a result of due influence uses a person's free will, informed consent and this uses our own choice about the influence as well as you have the right to question and leave the influence attempt.

One example would be TV advertising because you have the free will to choose whether or not to listen or care about this advert. As well as you can easily leave the advert and ignore the influence or persuasion attempt.

On the other end of influence, you have undue influence. This uses deceptive and manipulative tactics where you aren't allowed to question and your inner voice is suppressed. These types of influences include fear, coercion, control isolation and enslavement.

In addition, undue influence can be subtle like a cult leader giving you an illusion of control and informed control. With other examples including being abused by hypnosis and neurolinguistic programming.

Although, it's another sad truth that sometimes cults use overt and extreme types of undue influence. For instance, kidnapping and torture.

Overall, all undue influence is destructive and nothing good ever comes from it. Like, mind control and thought reform.

Cult Psychology and Leaders:

Whilst we'll look at the idea of the iconic cult leader in the next chapter, we need to talk about it now because we're still working on the basics.

Consequently, these leaders want people who are obedient to their rules and to the leader themselves. They don't want to be questioned or disrespected.

As a result, cult leaders look for a way to break people and this can be done in a few different ways.

Such as some leaders want and break people by making them willingly work for hours for little or no pay, and these leaders can make people willing slaves.

On the other hand, authoritarian religious cults often use members for labour trafficking.

On the whole, it doesn't really matter how or why a cult leader breaks or recruits a person. Due to when the mind is controlled, people are willing to suffer for the good of the group and leader. All whilst appearing happy.

Since the happiness of the members comes from their good performance within the group along with elitist thinking believing that they know the 'truth' or the best way to live.

Therefore, strict obedience is a requirement of cults and the members are manipulated by fear, guilt and may be stuck with no way out. (More on that later!)

<u>Identity Change:</u>

Earlier I mentioned how the suppression of a person's identity and I need to stress that undue influence does not erase a person's old identity from before they were recruited into the cult.

Instead the undue influence creates a new identity to suppress this older identity.

In addition, after different manipulation types, the process of creating a new identity is done step by step by formal indoctrination sessions. As well as informally by members, videos, movies, publication, media, games and media be it digital or social.

And if we horribly oversimplify the process, it is mainly behaviour modification that makes a person become a cult member. With some of the behaviour modification techniques including thought, control of their environment, isolation and restricted access to the others as well as rewards and punishment.

Then the new identity is reinforced, and the old identity is suppressed.

<u>Lasting Effects</u>

To wrap up this chapter on cult psychology basics, we need to talk about the entire reason why cults are awful, horrific things because they have long lasting effects that can destroy lives even after the cult is over.

As a result of the cult's use of prolonged and intense coercive persuasion and influence can cause a person to experience identity disturbance. This is essentially a person's inability to have major components of the self, self-esteem and other important concepts that allow us to know who we are and our purpose.

Leading to the common after-effects of:

- Depression

- Extreme identity confusion
- Panic and anxiety attacks
- Psychosomatic symptoms (headaches, backaches, skin problems and asthma)
- Distrust of self and others
- Anger, guilt and shame
- Decision-making dependency
- Sleep disorders/nightmares
- Eating disorders
- Loss of life meaning or purpose
- Fear and phobias
- Fear of intimacy and commitment
- Grieving loss of friends and family
- Delusions and paranoia
- Post-traumatic stress disorder (PTSD)

Overall, being a part of a cult has lots of horrible and dangerous side effects and this is one of the reasons why I want to write this book. Not only so I can learn about cults, but so we can all learn how cults work and hopefully avoid them if we have the unfortunate event of meeting one.

DANGEROUS CULT LEADERS: A PERSONALITY PSYCHOLOGY LOOK AT CULTS

Continuing with our look at the basics of cult psychology, we now need to consider what makes a cult leader dangerous?

Since when it comes to cult leaders, the question is never "When Is a Cult Leader 'Good Or 'Bad'?" because this is way too broad and subjective.

As a result, the true question is when is a cult leader pathological or a danger to others?

And if we think about this for a moment or two, I tend to think of the typical cult leader as dangerous (and yes this is completely influenced by my own representations of cults in my fiction books) because they have an army of mind controlled followers and the cult leader is a crazy, zealot who wanted to rule the world.

Okay whilst not everything in that paragraph is perfect or correct, we get the general idea about cult leaders being dangerous. Because they've got a group of mind controlled followers and it is the cult leader that has harmed these followers.

In addition, here's a list of dangerous cult leaders and I'm sure you've heard of most of them in some form or another from the news or public memory.

- Jim Jones (Jonestown Guyana)
- David Koresh (Branch Davidians)
- Stewart Traill (The Church of Bible Understanding)
- Charles Manson
- Shoko Asahara (Aum Shinrikyo)
- Joseph Di Mambro (The Order of the Solar Temple also known as the Ordre du Temple Solaire)
- Marshall Heff Applewhite (Heaven's Gate
- Bhagwan Rajneesh (Rajneesh Movement)
- Warren Jeffs (polygamist leader)

Personally, before I started researching this book I'd only ever heard of Charles Manson because he died in 2017 so I saw it on the news. Then I heard of Koresh when there was a TV drama done on the standoff between him and the FBI.

Another great and very disturbing example is in 1997, a former music professor called Applewhite managed to convince 38 people to commit suicide with him by placing plastic bags and purple cloths over their heads and they wore Nike trainers on their feet.

They did this ritualistic suicidal in an effort to reach a UFO hiding behind a Comet designated Hale-Bopp.

Afterwards, this UFO was meant to take them by a thing they called Heaven's Gate to an unspecified interplanetary reward.

And as a final extremely horrific note, Nike is Greek for victory so presumably these people thought they would achieve victory over something by wearing trainers. Is that it?

I guess that's half the fun of cult psychology, trying to understand why cults behave the way they do!

Additionally, this sounds exactly like something I would have done in one of my books and in fact I did do a mass ritualistic suicide short story a few years ago.

My fiction aside, this is just plain weird and this really emphasises the need for two things. One- to understand the cognitive processes between cult behaviour which we'll look at in three chapters later in the book.

Two- we need to fully understand what makes a cult leader dangerous and have the power to convince 38 different people to kill themselves with him.

What Makes a Cult Leader Dangerous?

After looking at why cult leaders can be so dangerous to themselves and others, let's look at what makes a cult leader dangerous.

It all tends to come down to a set of traits the cult leader has and it is these traits that make them a danger to themselves have others. As well as it's how they use these traits.

Furthermore, this is why personality psychology is useful because it gives us a set of traits to examine cult leaders with. Please see Personality Psychology and Individual Differences for more information.

For example, all cult leaders tend to be extremely narcissistic, and this personality trait by itself doesn't make a person a danger to others. It's how they use narcissism for lack of a better term that makes it dangerous.

As a result of cult leaders have an overabundant belief that they're special as well as they are the only ones who had the answers, and they have to be revered by other people. With these people being obedient and perfectly loyal to the leader.

Also the cult leader values themselves and purposefully devalues other people around them.

Naturally, you might have thought because of all these negative traits and how horrible these cult leaders are to be around. You might have thought no one would want to associate with them.

Well it turns out despite all these negative traits, the cult leaders still had no trouble attracting the type of people who would overlook these negatives.

Furthermore, there are a lot of other factors and personality traits cult leaders possess. Thus, there's a list of first warning signs as designed by a former FBI agent who created this list from his own studies and those of other people.

Meaning just as I said in my Criminal Profiling book, this type of research done by the FBI is hardly ever empirical and it lacks scientific rigour. So, please do not take this as a psychology (scientific) approved list of cult leader traits. But Navarro did incorporate findings from actual studies so it is better than a lot of FBI research.

However, I've decided to include it because whilst it isn't the be all and end all of traits, it's definitely comprehensive as well as I hope you find it useful.

Consequently, if a person has a lot of features

from the list then it's likely they are hurting those around them.

1. Requires excessive admiration from their followers and people outside the group.
2. They're arrogant and haughty in their behaviour or attitude.
3. Preoccupied with their fantasies of unlimited power, success, or brilliance.
4. Exploitative of others by asking for their money or that of relatives. Meaning others are out at financial risk.
5. Has a sense of entitlement—expecting to be treated as special at all times. This allows them to break laws and bend the rules.
6. Demands blind, unquestioning obedience from followers.
7. They have a grandiose idea of who they are and what they can achieve.
8. Sex is a requirement with adults and underage adults as part of a ritual or rite.
9. They take sexual advantage of the members.
10. Hypersensitive to how they're perceived as well as seen by others.
11. Makes members confess their sins or faults, publicly subjecting them to ridicule or humiliation while revealing exploitable weaknesses of the cult member.
12. Ignores the needs of others. This includes their emotional, financial, biological and physical needs.
13. Is frequently boastful of accomplishments.

14. Doesn't seem to feel guilty for anything they do wrong nor do they apologize for their actions.
15. Publicly devalues others as being incapable, inferior or not worthy.
16. Haughtiness, grandiosity, and the need to be controlling is part of their personality.
17. Hates to be embarrassed or fail publicly. Then when they do fail they act out in rage.
18. Habitually puts down others as inferior because of course only they're superior.
19. Has insisted on always having the best of anything (house, car, jewellery, clothes) even when others are relegated to lesser facilities, amenities, or clothing.
20. Behaves as though people are objects to be used, manipulated or exploited for personal gain.
21. Refers to non-members or non-believers as "the enemy."
22. Needs to be the centre of attention and does things to distract others to ensure that they're being noticed. For instance by using overdramatic speech, arriving late, making dramatic entrances and wearing exotic clothes.
23. Treats others with contempt and arrogance.
24. Rageful when criticised.
25. Is superficially charming.
26. Believes themselves to be omnipotent.
27. Has "magical" answers or solutions to problems.

28. Acts imperious at times, not wishing to know what others think or desire.
29. Deeply offended when there are perceived signs of boredom, of being slighted or being ignored.
30. Believes that they are a deity or a chosen representative of a deity.
31. Has a certain coldness about them that makes others worry about who this person really is and or whether they really know the leader.
32. "Rigid," "unbending," or "insensitive" describes how this person thinks.
33. Constantly assessing people to determine people that are a threat or people who revere him.
34. Believes they possess the answers and solutions to world problems.
35. The word "I" dominates their conversations as well as they're oblivious to how often they reference themself.
36. Monitors and/or restricts contact with family or outsiders.
37. Seems to be highly dependent on tribute and adoration as well as they will often *fish* for compliments.
38. Has isolated members of their sect from contact with family or the outside world.
39. Only to know ID obverse and validate.
40. Conceals background or family, which would disclose how plain or ordinary they are.
41. Uses enforcers or sycophants (think a teacher's pet or an intense flatter who does

this to gain an advantage) to ensure that the other members or believers comply with the leader.

42. Sees self as *unstoppable* and perhaps has even said so.

43. Has taken away followers' freedom to travel, live their own life, to leave the cult as well as liberty.

44. Tries to control how others think, view, read and what they do.

45. Works the least but demands the most.

46. Doesn't think there is anything wrong with them and in fact sees themselves as a person who is destined for greatness or they go through martyrdom.

47. Believe themselves to be perfect or blessed by a higher power.

Wow, that was a very long but interesting list. Therefore, after reading that I hope you can start to see the different dangerous combinations of personality traits a cult leader has and how they decide to use it. Due to perfectionism, narcissism amongst others aren't too problematic but when the leader wants to control others and dominant them. Then this is an entirely different matter.

Overall, I want to end this chapter by reminding you that whilst some of these traits or features don't seem scary. If a person disrespects, questions or challenges the cult leader, their insecure self-esteem will kick in and the consequences will most surely be dire for the cult member. And whilst a cult leader might be happy and seemingly perfect, they always hurt those around them even if the cult members don't realise it.

HOW DO NARCISSISTS USE CULT LEADER TACTICS TO CONTROL OTHERS?

Originally, I did this chapter as an episode on The Psychology World Podcast and it proved extremely popular and this episode was what made me commit to the idea of doing a cult psychology book.

Furthermore, this is a great chapter that continues on from our look at dangerous cult leaders because this explains the narcissism angle in a lot more depth.

I hope you find it useful!

**

People high in narcissism have very high self-esteem but it comes from an insecure place. Meaning when their self-esteem is threatened, this causes them to become defensive and hostile.

As a result, they try to influence and control others around them so other people don't threaten their self-esteem.

In fact, the tactics narcissists use to control and manipulate others have a lot of similarities with cult leaders.

Leading us onto the topics below.

Act Larger Than Life

It shouldn't surprise you that narcissists and cult leaders both act larger than life. Since this seems them seem wonderful with innate goodness and they have special knowledge that nobody knows about. As well as they believe that nobody is above them.

For cult leaders, this makes sure the cult members don't question them.

For narcissists, acting larger than life means the people around them don't threaten their self-esteem because they're special and gifted with secret knowledge.

Questioning Is Not Tolerant

In cults, questioning is horrified because if you question the cult, its leader and its purpose. Then you will quickly become ostracised and socially excluded. Because in the eyes of the cult, you've committed heresy, since how dare you question the all-knowing leader!

As a result, narcissists can use the same trick because if they exclude or become rageful at people who question them. Then the people around them will know not to question the narcissist and this gives the narcissist some level of control over their behaviour.

Additionally, the reason why questioning is so terrible for narcissists is because this is a direct threat to their unsecure self-esteem. Because you could be implicitly implying in your questions that they're wrong and they don't know what they're talking about. This will almost certainly decrease their self-esteem.

Lies Are Repeated So Often

With the cult leader being in such high regards and never ever being in the wrong. This means they repeat their lies so often that the cult member believes it.

Therefore, narcissists can do the same. All they need to do is keep telling those around them the same lies and how wonderful they are, and over time the people around them will start to believe it as the truth.

Their Righteousness Justifies the Means

Continuing on with the fact that the cult leader is perceived to be righteous and almost divine in some cases. It should come as no surprise, and you only need to look at some cults in the past 50 years to see this, that cults take part in some activities that normal people will shunt. Because it goes against their moral and ethical code.

Yet the reason why the cult members don't have a problem with this is because the cult leader says it's fine. Thus, the cult members believe it must be okay because the leader said so.

Additionally, if we think about it narcissists do some immoral behaviours at times. For instance, shouting, screaming and occasionally attacking people that threaten their self-esteem.

But if the narcissist has control and influence over those around them then these other people will most probably deem their behaviour as reasonable.

Meaning the narcissist's righteousness justifies the end.

<u>Independence Is Punished</u>

A while ago, I was reading an article on the psychology of cults on Psychology Today and I remember this point being raised in one way or another. The writer of the article showed the point perfectly because when she was invited into a cult and she wanted to socialise. The cult leader moaned at her because *she was interfering with God's time.*

Consequently, cult members are meant to be dedicated to the cult and they are meant to be one with the cult.

Otherwise, they are punished for their independence. This punishment can include social exclusion and ostracism and people prefer to keep social bonds even bonds that are bad for us. (Psychology of Relationships)

Finally, narcissists can control others around them using this trick because if the narcissist punishes someone for not being devoted to them. Then this could cause the narcissist to have stronger influence and control over this person.

PART TWO:
THE COGNITIVE PSYCHOLOGY
AND
SOCIAL PSYCHOLOGY
OF CULTS

CULT COGNITION AND COGNITIVE DISSONANCE

After looking at a lot of basics we know about cult influence, cult leaders and more. But how does cognitive psychology apply to cults?

So now we turn our attention towards mental processes with a dash of social psychology too.

Therefore, most adults know fiction isn't real. Everything that happens in fiction doesn't actually happen in real life and considering some of my fiction books, I'm extremely happy about that!

And because most adults know this difference between fact and fiction, this proposes an extremely interesting question. Because how do cult leaders convince people to believe in a fantasy realm or a weird cognitive landscape that isn't based in reality?

I know this is quite hard to imagine so one way to look at it is try to imagine Middle Earth from Lord of the Rings as being a real place. You just can't do it. You can't imagine orks, elves and little hobbits walking about or doing battle.

To answer this book, we need to look at cults from a social, clinical and cognitive psychology standpoint. As well as whilst this is an extremely complex question to answer because our understanding is at the beginning. For the purposes of this book, we'll look at three main cognitive explanations for cult behaviour.

These will be cognitive dissonance, group psychology and Dissociation. Also I know cognitive dissonance and group psychology are mainly social psychology topics but one of the great things about psychology is there is so much overlap between different subfields.

Cognitive Dissonance and Cults

As I explain in Social Psychology, Festinger et al (1956) created the term cognitive dissonance after one of his experiments that found people went through psychological distress and entered an uncomfortable state when their behaviours and attitudes didn't match. That's the general definition.

In terms of cult psychology, cognitive dissonance is the tendency to overvalue anything we're invested into too much. Be it time, money, emotional energy and more.

It basically means the more you have invested in something, the more you're going to like it. Regardless of how logical it is.

This can be seen in the Kerch (fake name) cult example. Where she apparently got a message from an alien planet warning her most of Earth's population would be wiped out by a flood on the 21st December 1954.

Leading her to start building her own cult and getting thousands of other people to believe in it. And as the world was ending her followers ended their careers, sold their houses, cars and even ended relationships.

Personally, I would love to know how those conversations went!

Overall, these beliefs had costed them dearly so they wanted, no actually needed this message to be true.

But when the flood day came and the world wasn't wiped out, the followers grew in their devotion even more.

Of course this makes no sense what so ever but this increase in devotion happened because Kerch explained she had received a message from God explaining that their devotion made him decide not to cause the flood.

Of course, this increase in devotion seems silly but it makes 'sense' if you look at it through a cognitive dissonance viewpoint.

Due to with these cult members paying invested so much in the cult and their beliefs. After all, most of them only had the cult left with them selling their houses, ending their jobs and ending relationships. These cult members were cut off from the rest of the world.

Therefore, they had to believe the messages were true, because can you believe how bad you would feel if you ruined your life for a lie?

That would destroy their self-esteem, positive self-image and their mental health would be gone.

Overall, it's much easier to convince yourself you're right and the messages are true than to admit they aren't.

However, Festinger's methods and his reliance on only the cognitive dissonance viewpoint have been criticised.

For a few different reasons but the main one is not everyone agrees with his interpretation of the results, as well as he focused exclusively on the cognitive dissonance angle.

Whereas in reality there were other processes going on including the other two we'll look at.

This is why I'm a massive fan of theory triangulation where you use different theories to understand your results. Because this reduces your bias and it increases the creditability of your results.

In addition, the belief in this rather extreme cult wasn't because people in the 1950s were stupid because the same results can be applied today.

As a result of Sharps et al (2013) studied the Mayan Calendar End of the World belief saying the world was meant to end on 21st December 2012. The researchers found 10% of the population thought the end of the world would definitely happen.

Of course nothing did, but this didn't matter to a lot of people. Because after nothing happened at all 10% still believed it would definitely happen. (Sharps et al, 2014)

Which I agree makes no sense because the belief clearly states the world would end on the 21st December 2012. So how could it still happen past that date?

The Takeaway:

On the whole at the end of this chapter, I think it's great and concerning to some extent that our physical reality has nothing on cognitive dissonance and other psychological dynamics as determinants of human behaviour.

Since it is these psychological dynamics that can morph our reality and make us believe things that are impossible in the real world.

Overall, cognitive dissonance maintains and even enhances cult beliefs. But how doesn't group psychology play a role?

CULT COGNITION AND GROUP PSYCHOLOGY

The second part of our cognitive psychology journey as we try to understand how our mental processes influence cult behaviour, we need to tap into the great cross-over between cognitive and social psychology as we look at group psychology.

Whilst I talk a LOT more about group psychology and other social psychology topics in Social Psychology: A Guide To Social and Cultural Psychology, this should still be easy to understand.

Conformity

Definitely one of social psychology's best researched area and some of the experiments are great. For example, Asch (1951, 1952, 1956) investigated conformity within our social groups by (in short) getting a participant in a group of confederates to say which line on a piece of paper best matched the other lines on the paper. Then on some trials the confederates all said the wrong answer and amazingly enough the participant said the same wrong answer, despite them knowing it was wrong.

Therefore, it shows the power of conformity because as Asch said himself young people are willing to call white, black. And I completely agree, conformity is amazing.

In addition, whilst there are of course criticism of Asch's work, the reasonable interpretation is very clear as well as it links to cults very clearly too.

As a result of people have a deep seated desperate need to be accepted by others.

In terms of cult psychology, this is useful to know because it helps to explain why people go along with the absurd beliefs of a cult. They want to be accepted by others. As well as these tendencies dramatically increase if the group of the cult has a leader.

Obedience:

However, conformity isn't the only great example of social psychology that applies to cults because obedience is a very important concept. And it's a great area of social psychology to look at because of

Milgram.

If you don't know who Milgram is I really do recommend you get any textbook or my own book on Social Psychology because Milgram was a very interesting person.

Nonetheless, in short, Milgram (1965, 1975) got participants to take part in what they thought was a learning experiment. In reality it was an experiment on obedience where the participants were the teachers and they gave the learner (a confederate) an electric shock increasing in voltage each time they got an answer wrong to 250 volts.

Also when the participant didn't want to shock the learner any more the authority figure (the experimenter) prompted them to continue. The participants obeyed and an extremely high percentage of the participants got to the full 450 volts.

Interestingly, we can apply these results to cults because the participants still obeyed Milgram despite him not harming the participant. Which in this case can be thought of as a cult member.

Showing the power of a cult leader or authority figure over their members. This can help to explain the power over the cult that a Messiah. For example, Charlie Manson, or any other cult leader or even Hilter could be considered a Messiah judging by the reverence his soldiers showed him.

What makes this interesting is it shows that people might (and probably would) kill others, themselves and perform other horrific actions to conform and obey their charismatic leader.

This has happened plenty of times before in history.

Hope:

On the whole, whilst humans are a conformist species which does tend to obey. There is still hope because humans have extremely powerful cognitive processes. Which we can use to resist the impulses which drive cultic and obedient behaviour.

Another reason for this is because of individual differences. With these differences meaning some people just don't get along with the cultic crowd.

Personally, I'm very happy about that fact and I wanted to explicitly say that the reason why this social psychology topic is mixed up in a cognitive psychology section is because whilst conformity and obedience are social processes. They're still choices and people are required to make a choice about their actions. Which firmly pulls these two areas under the remit of cognitive psychology.

Yet I wonder how dissociation applies to cults?

DISSOCIATIVE RESPONSES, SUPERNATURAL BELIEFS SYSTEMS AND HOW WE HELP THESE PEOPLE?

Moving onto the last chapter of our cult cognition section, we know that our obedience, conformity and cognitive dissonance can impact a cult's behaviour but there is a final factor we'll look at now.

Therefore, humans are very social creatures we all want to be with other people and as I discuss in my Psychology of Relationships book, we need to have relationships in our life or lots of negative things can happen.

Meaning humans need to be able to go along with the crowd and this demands a lot of cognitive processes, which the topic of Social Cognition looks at.

However, the question for this chapter is- if this

crowd is going towards the irrational, how does the human mind stick to the crowd?

Personally and you might agree with me, I cannot see myself ever wanting to believe in the irrational or just plain weird just to be in a social group. But sadly it does happen.

Dissociation

Leading us to the topic of dissociation and we aren't talking about Dissociative Identity Disorder. Instead we're looking at subclinical dissociation which is where anomalous perceptions of a person's experience come from a state of diffusion or unreality. (Sharps et al, 2014)

This is the dissociative state.

Furthermore, people experience it more than others and it can be devastating. With some examples of dissociative experiences including eyewitnesses of bigfoots, UFOs amongst other things.

It's important to note and make clear here that people who claim to see these things haven't necessarily got a mental health condition contrast to popular belief. These people are simply experiencing more senses of these things that aren't there.

This is where cults can come in because if we put these people in a social environment that is more persuasive. Then this can create a cognitive framework that has an emphasis on UFOs and myths. Causing people to see things that aren't really there. (Sharps et al, 2014)

This is exactly how cult thinking works.

As a result these cognitive frameworks are established to initiates novice cult members to believe in the cult's fantasy landscape.

With these dissociative processes being critical for helping believers understand the parts that don't make sense to them.

For example, if we stop here for a moment and consider the idea of the Heaven's Gate cult. We know that is a very weird idea because dissociation might allow members to understand how their leader could hear messages from aliens. Allowing them to understand and appreciate the *wisdom* in the Heaven's Gate idea.

Following this, the believers in the cult's ideas defend their beliefs through cognitive dissonance. (Sharps et al, 2020) This makes sense considering the members would have invested a lot into the cult so they want to be right and they want the cult to be righteous.

Nonetheless, this still doesn't explain how disassociation and the belief in these irrational ideas are allowed to happen in our cognitive system?

Well, the research shows that this happens because of our types of thinking. Since Sharps (2003) proposed a continuum of cognitive processing where people focus on the Gestalt processing (focusing on the hole and this involves rapid consideration of a situation without much consideration of the individual parts) at one end.

Then on the other end of the continuum, there's Feature-intensive processing. Whilst this is slower we focus more on the details of the situation.

Think of this as similar to the System 1 and 2 thinking by Kahneman.

With this continuum of thinking in mind, it's a lot easier to believe in the supernatural and bizarre in Gestalt processing. (Sharps et al, 2016) Since Feature Intensive thinking makes us confront the bizarre head on. Leading us to conclude the Messiah or cult leader is wrong.

Mini-Conclusion

Overall the past three chapters, we've looked at three main reasons for how our mental processes can help us fall for cults and their tactics.

From cognitive dissonance and our want for the cult to be true because we've invested so much into it.

To the group psychology processes that make us want to be accepted and obey an authority figure. To the cognitive processes of disassociation that allow us to believe in the supernatural in an easy to understand way.

How Can We Use This:

This was going to be in a separate chapter but that's no fun!

Consequently, the knowledge we've learnt from the past three chapters isn't just knowledge that we'll remember and we can never use it as a professional.

Due to Feature Intensive thinking can be used to reduce the tendency for a person to believe in the bizarre and irrational. By asking questions in Feature Intensive terms to reduce paranormal beliefs.

As a result of Feature Intensive processing leads to a reduction in Gestalt thinking, which sustains cult thinking and the belief in the bizarre.

But Festinger et al (1956) pointed out the source of the information can be questioned, but logic informed.

This makes sense because research to date shows that Feature Intensive thinking is only good and it only reduces Gestalt thinking when the person or cult member produces it themselves.

Telling people outright won't work.

Moreover, this emphasises the importance of asking specific questions that force the individual to consider issues in Feature Intensive terms and gets them to ask themselves to consider the real-world details of paranormal situations.

Thus, people generally respond with a lot more real-world thinking that tends to reduce vague, amorphous thinking that is necessary for cult mental processes when they think about the beliefs in Feature Intensive terms. (Sharps et al, 2000)

Conclusion

Overall, whilst psychology is only at the beginning at our cognitive understanding of cults. And the solution to cult cognition will require a lot more expertise in other areas of psychology than cognitive. At least we're starting to understand the mental underpinnings of cult behaviour and what to do about it.

CULTS AND THE SOCIAL PSYCHOLOGY OF THE SELF-SOOTHING PREJUDICE

This is another blog post I originally did for The Psychology World Podcast to celebrate Episode 50 of the show and this was the first time I had ever looked at cult psychology. It definitely sowed the seeds for my interest in cult psychology.

Personally, what I really like about the chapter below is it offers us another reason for why people are attracted to cults as well as it dips into personality psychology a little bit.

So, the blog post is below and I'll return at the end to link it to the rest of the book.

***

The Self-Soothing Prejudice:

This type of prejudice is when we discount a lot of people, mass or bulk discounting, so we can maintain peace of mind when we feel threatened.

For example, if you're attending a party and someone comes up to you. Making you feel threatened then quite naturally you might go:

You might be the best footballer in the school but I'm the best worker at my firm.

I don't know. It's just an example.

However, you get the idea because you discount those people who make you feel threatened by pointing out you're better at something else.

Overall, this type of prejudice is perfectly natural as it helps us to sustain our peace of mind.

Although, this self-soothing prejudice has a highly negative side when it reaches extreme levels.

As a result, the self-soothing prejudice corrupts us and if you engage in Absolute self-soothing prejudice then this truly as well as absolutely corrupts you.

This happens when we constantly bulk ourselves up with the self-soothing prejudice. You can easily compare it to using trump cards. Whenever you face a threat you use a trump card and instantly you have the winning answer to the threat.

And yet this self-soothing prejudice can be very damaging to us due to when we constantly and continually bulk ourselves up with the self-soothing prejudice, it becomes toxic to our friends and other relationships. Also, they may call you names. Like: you're a sociopath or psychopath.

Leading you to guess what, pulling out another trump card to show to yourself that you are far better than these name-callers.

Overall, these trump cards come from Cults.

Cults and The Self-Soothing Prejudice:

Interestingly, Cults give out trump cards to their members as part of their appeal and it has a lot of interesting effects on their members.

Nonetheless, the members take these trump cards so they can be better than everyone else, and they are willing to be brainwashed.

Although, the members come to the Cult because the Cult has discovered the 'truth' and everyone else believes in the lies. Yet the members fail to see that these trump cards are no different from other cults. Regardless of the Cult's 'truth'

Building upon this further, the trump cards allow

the members to become absolute in their perfection and their mistakes aren't mistakes as well as they become infallible. All to provide themselves with a fantasy break from the jealous anxiety of everyday life.

Over time this becomes addictive and engaging with the self-soothing prejudice and the trump card becomes more natural than rational thoughtfulness.

Overall, engaging in extremely high levels of self-soothing prejudice is very dangerous.

***

Linking this to the rest of the book, this links to a few different areas. For example, it offers up another explanation to why cult leaders are so narcissistic because they engage in high levels of the self-soothing bias. With them constantly needing to remind people and use these trump cards to show other people how amazing they are.

Moreover, it explains why cult members can end up joining cults because if people don't have the community, social support and defences to support themselves. Then these trump cards look very tempting because it would finally allow some cult members to defend themselves if they live in a bad situation.

WHY CULTS ARE MINDLESS: COST REQUIREMENTS, SUPERNATURAL BELIEF SYSTEMS AND OBEDIENCE

I'll fully admit this was a difficult chapter to know where to put because this chapter could easily go at the beginning and straight after the cult psychology basics. But I really wanted to put the chapter here because now we know about cult cognition and the basics of cult psychology, this foundation knowledge will allow us to understand the topic of the chapter a lot better.

As a result, Sosis and Bressler (2003) studied US communes (religious communities in this case) and they found that communes that are more demanding lasted for longer.

These larger sacrifices made the members more emotionally committed to the group. And this all comes back to cognitive dissonance since with these members investing so much into the group, they want it to be successful and they can't really afford for the cult to fail.

In terms of these sacrifices, the extremeness of them depended on the communes with some communes being very extreme by requiring members to be celibate and surrender all their worldly possessions. Other communes were not so demanding.

In addition, the great demand the cult leaders placed on their members lead to an increase in member cooperation and the commune's survival.

Practically speaking, if a commune had two costly requirements then they tend to fail within 10 years.

If a commune had 6 to 8 burdensome costs then these communes tended to survive for over 50 years.

As well as if a commune has 11 or over then the communes were still in business 60 years later.

In my opinion, this list of times and the costly requirement is a perfect example of cognitive dissonance in driving cult behaviour as we can clearly see the more a member invests in the cult. The more they want it to succeed.

However, these burdensome requirements only helped religious community groups stick together. Which offers us great insight into the social cohesive function of supernatural beliefs.

In terms of non-religious or secular communities, they were generally less stable with them generally lasting less than 10 years.

But what makes this even more interesting is it works the opposite for secular communities. Meaning the more costly the requirements and the more burdensome the group is, the quicker these secular cults fail. With the most demanding secular cults ending in less than a year.

Why?

The reason for this opposite way of working can be explained by sacrifice for each type of community is viewed differently by each type.

Due to the communes with their supernatural belief system can justify heavy memberships costs in terms of higher purpose. Since they're doing these heavy costs so they can know the truth of the universe, be taken to heaven, to be spared by a flood and more.

Subsequently, without these beliefs, the members start to ask themselves is the membership cost too high. Leading them to possibly conclude they're being exploited by the leader of the group. Then the next logical step is to leave.

Inequality Between Members:

This is a very interesting next section because in general (and yes I'm being extremely general here) in western society we tend to be fairly against inequalities between members of society.

However, in cults, the members can be perfectly okay with inequality because when backed up by a religious belief system, communes can tolerate a lot of inequality.

With this most easily can be illustrated by the permissible sexual behaviour of cult leaders and their uncaring attitudes towards social inequalities within the cult.

One fairly famous example is the celibacy in secular commune would be destabilised by the free sexual expression of the leader.

Nonetheless, when you have people with a supernatural belief system then this could work if the members believe the leader is a divine being. Therefore, of course it's okay for the cult leader to have sex whilst the members remain celibate. Because they're divine and the members are pointless mortals.

Furthermore, this happened in real life with the David Koresh Cult that was wiped out in a fire in 1983 after a stand off with federal authorities near Waco, Texas.

Due to Koresh had access to all female members of the cult consistent with his divine station. But the other men had to be celibate.

Blind Obedience

Returning to our look at blind obedience, religious cults that survive for more than a few years are characterised by blind obedience.

Meaning this proposes a lot of difficult questions for friends, family, clinical psychologists as well as researchers, because why would these members want to surrender their autonomy in the first place?

Now in terms of psychology and wider human behaviour, cults aren't unusual in this regard because there are a lot of different situations or organisations that get people to give up small pieces of their autonomy for the good for the group. There are a few covert sections on this in Social Psychology in case you're interesting.

For example, the army and sport organisations with their byzantine (extremely detailed) rules as well as world religions and groupthink in political life. All follow this to varying degrees.

In addition, mindless obedience is good for the cult but it is never good for cult members. And this can be applied to entire countries because if citizens are mindless obedient to their Head of State, it's great for the Head. But very bad for its members.

Overall, the less inequality there is, the better quality of life everyone experiences.

HELPING PEOPLE TRAPPED IN CULTS

Moving onto the last chapter of the book, this should be a great chapter and it should be the most useful. But of course absolutely nothing in this book is any sort of official or professional advice.

Personally, I've been really looking forward to writing this chapter because we briefly touched on this topic in the last cognitive chapter. But now we get to dive deep or deeper in this amazing topic.

Therefore, we know cult leaders use deceptive tactics to recruit members into their cult as well as even rational, intelligent people can fall for cults.

Furthermore, if a member is extremely devoted to the cult they will happily cut off contact and relationships with people that are different from them and the cult's beliefs. And this is where this chapter comes in.

Techniques to Help

Regardless of the type of cult whether it's an authoritarian, political, religious, personality or another type of cult, the techniques to help remain the same.

Because if you're concerned for a person's wellbeing then don't argue with them, cut them off or call them names.

Instead you would need to try to engage respectfully, warmly and communicate regularly. Due to this serves as a way to help repair bridges that could help the member to start thinking more rationally. Then in time the cultic bubble will burst, as well as reality will return to them.

The former cult member, PhD, mental health counsellor and author Steven A. Hassan developed some great techniques to help people. With him emphasizing that helping a person is a process requiring love, patience and effort.

In addition, his first recommended tips are a person should research cults and mind control to allow them to become well informed. For example, learn about what communication strategies are most effective because as we saw in an earlier chapter arguing with logic doesn't work.

Subsequently, he stresses the need for building

rapport and trust with the member by rebuilding relationships, apologise and talk on common areas. But avoiding hot topics.

Moreover, he recommends that you can try to minimise or even remove the media that continually indoctrinate the person to only one point of view. And whilst this might only work with certain cults, the cult might indoctrinate their members through the media.

So you can make a pact to go on a media fast together. Not as a solution to fix them or their problem but as a fun thing to do.

Of course, you need to keep your end of the pact if this happens.

Things to Do *During* Your Conversations

Therefore, after you've rebuilt this relationship and you and the cult member are getting along well. Then he proposes doing the following things in conversations.

- Keep the conversations positive, productive and civil. Never get angry with them and stay resourceful. It's better to end the interaction than to say something counter-productive. It's better to return to the conversation at another time, rather than the person cutting off all communication out of anger or fear.

- Ask thought-provoking questions while being warm and curious. Be prepared to listen deeply. They will know if you have listened well if you can repeat back to them what they said. Be humble and open to hearing what they say.
- Use examples of cult leaders with similar qualities to their group's leader(s) and have conversations about it.
- Adopt a general tone of curiosity and interest in their positions. Pretend you're an impartial counsellor. Really try to *get inside* their beliefs.
- Try to get them to look at reality from many different perspectives. This can include many things.
- and how you miss it.
- Don't *"tell"* them anything. Help them to make discoveries on their own.
- Try to connect them with their authentic identity *before* these extreme beliefs. Remind them of your past experiences together. Talk about the connection you once had
- Teach them about indoctrination and mind control. Use examples for which they have no attachment.
- Ask a question and then wait for them to think and respond. Be patient. You do not need to fill the silence.
- Share feelings and perceptions, not judgments. Use "I feel" statements. Don't

claim to be "right." Stick to what your perception is when reflecting back to them.

However, I want to add that you need to understand that an abundance of facts just will not help you necessarily because you don't want to overwhelm them with information. Especially, if the information attacks the leader of the cult's doctrines. Because then cognitive dissonance and the member's other defence mechanisms kick in.

Overall, whilst I purposefully kept this brief to some extent and nothing in this book is any sort of professional or official advice. I hope you found it interesting and it shows how the process of getting a cult member to change their beliefs is a long process.

Requiring patience because this is all a journey, and it sadly won't happen overnight. So if you are in this situation, please get professional help and don't get discouraged. People do leave cults in the end.

CONCLUSION

In conclusion, I really hope you've enjoyed this book. I know I have. I've really enjoyed exploring cults and cult psychology and all the different ways that they work.

From the basics of cult psychology to why and how cult leaders are dangerous (and after some of the examples of real life cults, I never ever want to meet one!) to the cognition behind cults and most importantly how to help get people out of cults.

I think my two favourite parts of this book had to be how to help people get out of cults, which I'll reflect on in a moment.

But my second favourite part was the cognitive psychology sections because at university we're all taught the same standard areas of Cognitive Psychology. Such as: memory, thinking,
· metacognition amongst other types.

Therefore, when we get to apply cognitive psychology or any subfield of psychology to something new and exciting I too get extremely excited.

Because before I researched and wrote this book, I had no idea cognitive dissonance was related to cults. And to be honest, I hadn't heard of dissociation before outside of the personality disorder.

However, before I wrap up the book, I want to reflect on something I said in chapter 1. The reason why learning about cults is important is because it allows us to recognise these individuals and tactics in our own lives. Allowing us to defend and avoid these situations because as we've seen over the past few chapters once in a cult, it's difficult to leave and the aftereffects can be devastating.

So, I hope you've learnt something and enjoyed the book.

Have a great day and I'll see you in another book soon!

REFERENCES

https://www.psychologytoday.com/gb/blog/freedom-mind/202106/understanding-cults-the-basics

https://www.psychologytoday.com/gb/blog/spycatcher/201208/dangerous-cult-leaders

https://www.psychologytoday.com/gb/blog/the-forensic-view/202010/cults-and-cognition-programming-the-true-believer

https://www.psychologytoday.com/gb/blog/the-forensic-view/202010/cults-and-cognition-ii-programming-the-true-believer

https://www.psychologytoday.com/gb/blog/the-forensic-view/202011/cults-and-cognition-programming-the-true-believer

https://www.psychologytoday.com/gb/blog/freedom-mind/202104/the-definitive-guide-helping-people-trapped-in-cult

https://www.psychologytoday.com/gb/blog/tal
king-about-trauma/201502/ritual-abuse-cults-and-captivity

https://www.psychologytoday.com/gb/blog/am
bigamy/201807/why-people-become-narcissists-gaslighters-and-cult-members

https://www.psychologytoday.com/us/blog/nar
cissism-demystified/202103/9-ways-many-narcissists-behave-cult-leaders

Barber, N. (2012). Why atheism will replace religion: The triumph of earthly pleasures over pie in the sky. E-book

Sosis, R., & Bressler, E. (2003). Cooperation and commune longevity: A test of the costly signaling theory of religion. Cross-Cultural Research, 37, 211-239.

Newport, K. G. C. (2006). The branch Davidians of Waco: The history and beliefs of an apolalyptic sect. New York: Oxford University Press.

Wilkinson, R., & Pickett, K. (2010). The spirit level: Why greater equality makes societies stronger. New York: Bloomsbury Press.

Festinger, L. Reicken, H.W., & Schachter, S. (1956, reprinted 2011). *When Prophecy Fails*. Blacksburg, VA: Wilder Publications.

Sharps, M.J., Liao, S.W., & Herrera, M.R. (2013). It's the End of the World, and They Don't Feel Fine; The Psychology of December 21, 2012. *Skeptical Inquirer, 37,* 34-39.

Sharps, M.J., Liao, S.W., & Herrera, M.R. (2014). Remembrance of Apocalypse Past. *Skeptical Inquirer, 38,* 54-58.

Asch. S.E. (1955). Opinions and Social Pressure. *Scientific American, 193,* 31-35.

Milgram, S. (1974). *Obedience to Authority.* New York: Harper & Row.

Hoffer, E. (1951). *The True Believer: Thoughts on the Nature of Mass Movements.* New York: Harper and Brothers

Sharps, M.J. (2003). *Aging, Representation, and Thought: Gestalt and Feature-Intensive Processing.* New Brunswick NJ: Transaction.

Sharps, M.J., Liao, S.W., & Herrera, M.R. (2016). DIssociation and Paranormal Beliefs: Toward a Taxonomy of Belief in the Unreal. *Skeptical Inquirer, 40,* 40-44.

Sharps, M.J., Nagra, S., Hurd, S., & Humphrey, A. (2020). Magic in the House of Rain: Cognitive Bases of UFO 'Observations' in the Southwest Desert. *Skeptical Inquirer, 44,* 46-49.

https://freedomofmind.com/strategic-interactive-approach/

https://www.proquest.com/docview/2476570146/

Thinking, Fast and Slow by Daniel Kahneman (2013)

Thought Reform and the Psychology of Totalism: A Study of 'brainwashing' in China by Dr. Robert Jay Lifton

Combating Cult Mind Control: The Guide to Protection, Rescue and Recovery from Destructive Cults

Opening Our Minds: avoiding abusive relationships and authoritarian groups by Jon Atack

Social Psychology: A Guide to Social and Cultural Psychology by Connor Whiteley.

Psychology of Relationships: The Social Psychology of Friendships, Romantic Relationships, Prosocial Behaviour and More Third Edition by Connor Whiteley.

https://www.subscribepage.com/psychology
boxset

Thank you for reading.

I hoped you enjoyed it.

If you want a FREE book and keep up to date about new books and project. Then please sign up for my newsletter at www.connorwhiteley.net/

Have a great day.

CHECK OUT THE PSYCHOLOGY WORLD PODCAST FOR MORE PSYCHOLOGY INFORMATION!

AVAILABLE ON ALL MAJOR PODCAST APPS.

About the author:

Connor Whiteley is the author of over 30 books in the sci-fi fantasy, nonfiction psychology and books for writer's genre and he is a Human Branding Speaker and Consultant.

He is a passionate Warhammer 40,000 reader, psychology student and author.

Who narrates his own audiobooks and he hosts The Psychology World Podcast.

All whilst studying Psychology at the University of Kent, England.

Also, he was a former Explorer Scout where he gave a speech to the Maltese President in August 2018 and he attended Prince Charles' 70th Birthday Party at Buckingham Palace in May 2018.

Plus, he is a self-confessed coffee lover!

All books in 'An Introductory Series':

BIOLOGICAL PSYCHOLOGY 3RD EDITION

COGNITIVE PSYCHOLOGY THIRD EDITION

SOCIAL PSYCHOLOGY- 3RD EDITION

ABNORMAL PSYCHOLOGY 3RD EDITION

PSYCHOLOGY OF RELATIONSHIPS- 3RD EDITION

DEVELOPMENTAL PSYCHOLOGY 3RD EDITION

HEALTH PSYCHOLOGY

RESEARCH IN PSYCHOLOGY

A GUIDE TO MENTAL HEALTH AND TREATMENT AROUND THE WORLD- A GLOBAL LOOK AT DEPRESSION

FORENSIC PSYCHOLOGY

THE FORENSIC PSYCHOLOGY OF THEFT, BURGLARY AND OTHER

OTHER SHORT STORIES BY CONNOR WHITELEY

Blade of The Emperor

Arbiter's Truth

The Bloodied Rose

Asmodia's Wrath

Heart of A Killer

Emissary of Blood

Computation of Battle

Old One's Wrath

Puppets and Masters

Ship of Plague

Interrogation

Sacrifice of the Soul

Heart of The Flesheater

Heart of The Regent

Heart of The Standing

Feline of The Lost

Heart of The Story

The Family Mailing Affair

Defining Criminality

The Martian Affair

A Cheating Affair

The Little Café Affair

GARRO: MISTRESS OF BLOOD

GARRO: BEACON OF HOPE

GARRO: END OF DAYS

Winter Series- Fantasy Trilogy Books

WINTER'S COMING

WINTER'S HUNT

WINTER'S REVENGE

WINTER'S DISSENSION

Miscellaneous:

THE ANGEL OF RETURN

THE ANGEL OF FREEDOM

Companion guides:

BIOLOGICAL PSYCHOLOGY 2ND EDITION WORKBOOK

COGNITIVE PSYCHOLOGY 2ND EDITION WORKBOOK

SOCIOCULTURAL PSYCHOLOGY 2ND EDITION WORKBOOK

ABNORMAL PSYCHOLOGY 2ND EDITION WORKBOOK

PSYCHOLOGY OF HUMAN RELATIONSHIPS 2ND EDITION WORKBOOK

HEALTH PSYCHOLOGY WORKBOOK

FORENSIC PSYCHOLOGY WORKBOOK

Audiobooks by Connor Whiteley:

BIOLOGICAL PSYCHOLOGY

COGNITIVE PSYCHOLOGY

SOCIOCULTURAL PSYCHOLOGY

ABNORMAL PSYCHOLOGY

PSYCHOLOGY OF HUMAN
RELATIONSHIPS

HEALTH PSYCHOLOGY

DEVELOPMENTAL PSYCHOLOGY

RESEARCH IN PSYCHOLOGY

FORENSIC PSYCHOLOGY

GARRO: GALAXY'S END

GARRO: RISE OF THE ORDER

GARRO: SHORT STORIES

GARRO: END TIMES

GARRO: COLLECTION

GARRO: HERESY

GARRO: FAITHLESS

GARRO: DESTROYER OF WORLDS

GARRO: COLLECTION BOOKS 4-6

GARRO: COLLECTION BOOKS 1-6

Business books:

TIME MANAGEMENT: A GUIDE FOR
STUDENTS AND WORKERS

LEADERSHIP: WHAT MAKES A GOOD
LEADER? A GUIDE FOR STUDENTS
AND WORKERS.

BUSINESS SKILLS: HOW TO SURVIVE
THE BUSINESS WORLD? A GUIDE FOR
STUDENTS, EMPLOYEES AND
EMPLOYERS.

BUSINESS COLLECTION

GET YOUR FREE BOOK AT:
WWW.CONNORWHITELEY.NET

CPSIA information can be obtained
at www.ICGtesting.com
Printed in the USA
LVHW081922271221
707271LV00002B/32

9 781915 127259